AF492333

ALSO BY ANTONIA WANG:

IN ENGLISH:

Love Bites: Poetry & Prose
In the Posh Cocoon: Poetry and Bits of Life
Hindsight 2020: Brief Reflections on a Long Year
Palette: Love Poems and Painted Words
Things I Could Have Said in One Line But Didn't:
Poems on Love, Relationships and Existentialism
Taste of Salt: Poems on Love and Life
Healing (From Everything, All the Time):
Poetry and Vignettes

IN SPANISH:

Retrospectiva 2020: Reflexiones breves
sobre un año largo
Matices: Poemas de amor y paisajes del alma
Rincones barridos: Poesías del interior

THE CONSTANT

POEMS ON HOLDING, LEAVING, AND BECOMING

ANTONIA WANG

Sometimes the poem is for the poet.
Sometimes it's for someone unborn,
who will one day seek shelter
under the same willow.

Contents

Untitled haiku appear on pages 30, 38, 102, 106, and 118.

Part I. Measuring the Hollow

I rise, a sage post-regression.

— *Under Your Gravity*

Alive Enough

Everything you see is real,
though, in theory, this is a dream:
Maya. Gaia. Holograms
beamed into the Matrix.

A website insists you're alive,
even though you barely feel so.
It takes more sugar to sweeten
corn muffins these days,
more sunlight to freckle a face.

My body aches for weeks after "a cold"
though we both know what I really had.
It takes more than a virus
to kill me now. Dissonance
tugs my limbs in opposite extremes.

Inertia weighs more than love,
more even than hate.
It takes the sky bawling to refill a river—
compassion to undress madness,
magic to undig from sadness.

Gathered Here

Harm-free under the stars,
a graveyard, self-guided tour
among friends and fallen leaves.
A toddler's tomb—we gather,
more curious than sorrowful,
as if time congeals after death:
two years, same as ninety.
One could cram
lifetimes into a closed-eyed kiss,
millennia into a lullaby.
Infinity is so fragile—
it flushes away
in the rush of a moment.

Measuring the Hollow

I alone can fill this house,
with mementos brushed in sepia.
Once, I feared the silence—
the droning stridulation
of loneliness, the clock's
relentless tick, tallying
each second left, unyielding
as a heart that won't forget.

I measure the giant bookshelf
that will claim the new space.
It alone can fill a house
with whispers of a lived-in life—
characters brimming
with the vellichor of old things
no one can bear to leave behind.

Carving Space

The line breaks intentionally,
in awkward places—I stand alone,
my feet too wide on its trace.
I've written poems of the past,
though they foretell the future.
"The Things We Carry" rings
like a bell through this empty room.

Leaving, like giving birth,
precedes a necessary emptiness—
a sadness for what once was:
a temporary space, filling
and growing within you—
not as you,
but as something additional.

A Stager's Eye

Someone else knows best
how to arrange my life—
a stager, whose hands
group disparate objects
into coherent themes.
The wooden lighthouse from Florida,
seashells from an Australian beach
(edges worn like old intentions),
an elephant whose gilded trunk
must reach toward the door, inviting fortune.
Balance to please the eye:
metal and wood, crystal and books—
as if harmony could be ordered
with a stranger's touch.
A fake plant where light can't reach,
hefty vases that hold nothing…
I see it now—how I could have
lived more beautifully,
more elegantly, in a home
someone else will buy, only to unload
their own mismatched fragments.

Picking Up the Pieces

Re(membered) by long,
invisible fingers—
A clump of pink flesh,
dislocated bones.
Who am I under this blanket,
wobbly, as I stand unaided—
no key to my anatomy.
Will I survive,
with my spine beneath my feet?
Will my skull unfold
from the cradle of my navel,
When the sky splits open
to a remade azure?

Self-Doubt

I. The Little Man
What if I've been wrong about things,
about the little Ikea mannequin
resting on my bookshelf?
What if his exultant pose, set by me,
is varnished sadness? What if I lower his head,
droop his arms, make his legs limp?
What if I leave him here, alone, when I leave?

II. The Bigger Man
What if I've noticed everyone but *him*,
the folded figure asleep under my blanket,
inhaling my exhales. His pulse, a ticking clock
so loud, I can't hear myself.
Does he live within me, or am I a fixture
on his stairway wall? Do my eyes move at all
when he stares at me?

III. Everything
What if I'm just wrong—about everything,
and everyone I meant to do right by?
About the honeysuckles I trimmed,
about pushing *her* to learn what she didn't want?
Wrong about where I am, how I love,
what I eat—about the very premise
of these fumbling lines.

Ice-Carved Resolutions

Bare skin as proof of love,
lace instead of fleece.
Dawn spills over
fawn-colored sheets.
Days like these,
friskier than my nerves—
no answers in books or eyes,
to the biting chill,
to the swallow's flight.

Uncertainty steeps
like morning tea,
lips puckered to bone china.
A cat sprawls across the vent,
blank as a fevered thought.
Short arms can't warm me
through layers of new flesh,
growing as I type these words—
rushing, like January,
to etch itself in frost,
to give the year meaning,
a bridge to nothing,
a bane to fleeting youth.

In the Interim…

I press a sharp pencil to a worn map,
trace the street we will call home.
Circle a school, a studio, a store—
landmarks that will shape a story.

I scrawl the names of strangers I'll meet,
shade a green mountain in charcoal
until the lead wears down to nothing,
until it smudges all it touches.

Still, there's time for one more scribble
on the yellow notebook with the smiling cat,
beneath medications I meant to check
for interactions and side effects.

This slogging chapter nears its end.
My fingers move faster than my eyes.
I have sprawled too wide in this yellowing page,
bathed too long in this swamp of murmurs.

Abridged List of Phobias

Why am I so scared?
A pin-drop startles me,
a falling leaf rattles me.
I jump at a sneeze,
bolt at a scream.
My heart, a Merengue drum,
is always on—pump, pump, pumping—
my veins, pulsing enemies of the present.
Noise pierces not my ears,
but my cellophane skin.
I do not bleed. I sweat.
Fear is not blood, but a brick wall
in the middle of an open field—
not a climbing wall, but one to crawl over
without a harness. I fear the absence of blue
over the pearl-white loneliness,
rivers that trickle for want of rain,
the milk chocolate avalanche of excess.
I fear maybes for their uncertainty,
forevers for their stone-set finality—
but mostly, I dread
the screeching halt of never.

As Within, So Without

Pointless still—
a misanthrope sinks into a park bench,
blinded to the world. Footfalls
press into the mud path.

A woman passes,
wearing the future like a sundress.
Ask her: Where is home,
when hunger stops? What does she see
when she looks through you?

Back home,
doors swing and shut—
unanswered as revolving questions.
She never met your eyes
when she passed.

Why search a stranger's gaze
for your reflection?
How did she know
not to mirror your emptiness?

park bench reverie
a ginger cat marks my leg
what I see owns me

Sadness, the Silent Temptress

She hums—to remind you she's there—
beautiful and bare-faced—reclining
on the sofa, beyond the reach of your gaze.
You walk past, ignoring her,
for there are layers to your rough skin,
and the current one breathes no sadness.
The skies dim to an atmospheric gloom.
Six months of penitence for each stolen ray
of sun. Who, so frail and pallid
could withstand any more?

She brushes her shiny tresses, unaged
like an unwavering promise.
And tomorrow, as she always does, she'll stare
at you through someone else's doleful eyes—
but you will know her pupils dilating to quiet
agony. This is her only freedom, expanding
in the warm dunes of carefully tended misery,
pretty and poised, like a desert primrose.

Wanting World

Oh mighty sun,
my ginger tyrant,
yolked puppet-master
of eyes and souls!

Circadian lord
of a sutured sky,
that old rag doll.

Sans your warmth I fold
like an unloved fetus
waiting, wet and wounded
in a stranger's womb.

Fed and housed,
I suck my thumb,
waiting to be born
into a wanting world.

Waiting for Groundhog Day

Two decoy owls
with their faux wisdom
stare through the grand room windows.
Senile suns doze in their eyes,
too distant to toast or brighten.

Below them, two pumpkins shiver—
flesh unscathed, seeds intact,
relics of a short-lived harvest.

Next door, Christmas lights still glow,
but storefronts have changed
to pastels and spring motifs.
I am caught in between:
a spotty warmth, a patient chill.

AstroCartography

Moving westward—
my left arm pulls
the rest of me toward him.
My destination, not a place,
though I was known to love a Bay,
frigid and fragile, fainting in the fog
of delayed summer—a mercy
for those whose inner frost
cracks under the weight of autonomy
no one really wants.

Is it true we wither
in the wrong city, the wrong season,
the wrong hands?
Do I breathe deeper where the air is drier,
where mountains duel plains of dullness—
where red is both color and topography;
where gold is true and sentient.
Do I get to thrive—under bluer skies?

Mile-High Downer

35

I've come to 16th Street,
lugubrious home of the homeless.
Today, they sit beneath
a warm roof in a nearby hotel.
Still, they own this place.
The birds are gone,
the bathrooms are locked,
their hushed vestige—a sonic tear.
Police guard the stores,
scattering crows.
I am here for a moment, a tourist
in their Arctic box—
hot chocolate in one hand.
In the other, a book I can't warm.

Here, Beyond

Don't claim me as the evening falls,
past the headlands, driving your car
to a parallel world.

Don't tally me among your scores—
soaring twilight, whispering breeze.
I exist beyond your fortunes,
near the shadowlands you dread.

Tremble, the woods, without my love,
warm with the borrowed heat
of a constant presence. Here—
feel my pulse in the passenger seat.

I never left, never truly lived.
Descend the ladder to yourself;
when you find you, you shall find me…
swinging on the cradling hammock.

Prayer of the Evergreen

Wax a dry leaf,
so it doesn't feed the sated soil.
Suspend a snowflake midair,
to keep its crystal intact.
Frame fire with steel—
we can't stand ambiguity.
Perpetuate loss,
for it's the pattern we know.

Stop the seasons, I'm evergreen.
Though my hair turns grey where I part it,
and the earth cracks where I step,
I dream of a heart
that can cope with beauty,
darkness, and pain—
without needing to grow,
or having to change.

watercolor rain
pastel tears stain my window
diluted world's splash

Immune to Change

Memory's hide and seek:
drawing forgotten faces,

sealed full lips
where a line should lead.

My strength is spent,
yet my legs still tread.

No reward in living,
no solace in death.

Taut skin, dull pulses
of squandered youth.

I've strayed so far
from my anchor's mark.

All is foreign,
all is new.

Hanging by a Thread

In this other life,
I wear the French silk scarf,
raw and alive,
(like real fabric should be).
My fingertips trace
the hand-sewn hems.

Somewhere, under the weave
of a simpler time, lies a girl—
her hands too weak to write
her own story, her palms
too sore to thread a needle
and lift it up
to burst the pent-up sky.

Morning's liquid pools
beneath the wall clock.
I hear tick-tocks as I swim
through the late summer silence.

Nothing has unraveled yet today.
But still, with weak, sore hands,
I clench the hems
of the French silk scarf
a little too tightly.

The Book Where the Muse Sleeps

The book where the muse sleeps
is down in the basement—one stair too far.
It is dark down there, now that I'm here.
It is dark up here too.

My cat sleeps against my tailbone.
His languor clashes with my wiggles.
The muse demands a silence I don't yet have.
Silence is a place, and I'm not there—
not today. The vent, the clock, the phone
all ping, buzz, tip, and tap.

A song in my radio head wants to be heard,
but hearing takes ears I no longer have,
and a hollow heart to gather its fruits like a basket.
Mine isn't hollow enough for harvest,
but spongy enough for droplets
that weigh it down—down, down...

There—
that's the lowliness that lures the muse,
and scatters the words like fruit.

Visions of a Newborn Night

A crying night crowns from the laboring moon.
Autumn sneaks quietly through an open window
into an unmade bed no one has slept in.
Billowing curtains, weightless as her silk gown.
Tsundoku sighs, its dust settling slow.
Stirring utopias wither, unlived. Captive words,
still bound to unanswered questions.
She sips the comfort of stories unread,
savoring the ache of an untrodden quest.

The veil is thinning, tactile and yet ethereal
for those acquainted with the dark.
To her, it was only ever a bride's
off-white tulle blusher, cloaking
her asymmetry on a day of perfection—
but never the outside. She can see,
bright as day, through the fog of drowsy trees,
eyes closing to a crow's lullaby,
an ATLAS comet tracing lazy arcs
across the chill of newborn shadows.

Part II. The Space Between Notes

Messy, uneven,
but they seem to hold.

— *I Know You Can Hear Me*

Under Your Gravity

What we love, we're bound to fear.
How else could we hear
the percussion of our pulse?
He calls me, and I turn—
too prompt to hide the sting.
I'm in love again, after all these years:
eons waking to the same sun,
half-dreaming through scattered zip codes.
Now I rise, a sage post-regression,
while time gives no clue to its ticking.
I fear to commit, even after the fact,
yet I act—eyes lowered, knees trembling,
ankles tied to the capricious moon.

In the Rising

Tired eyes see only blurry shapes,
sketched by the blunt tip of a wax pencil.
Rain—more mood than weather—
cold drops on thawing earth,
heaven's own self-applause.
Thus comes spring, the eve of a sigh
among violets—bold colors waking
before the heart grins.
I want you sweet on my morning bread,
fragrant and untoasted, exuding
gentle warmth at first touch,
and always ready to rise again.

The Constant

On the long arm of sentience
lives a moment,
burned and healed
like a third-world vaccine—
indelible fusion
of a nightmare-dream.
I sit within the river
that flows without choice,
unmoved by sheer will.

All is transient
except what stands still
in the void. You,
a boulder in that river,
softened by time's touch,
couldn't move even if you tried.
Eons after water dries to memory,
and my bones join the dust
in the blowing wind,
you'd remain.

And the River Grows

He strokes my hand with his thumb,
lingering, in amorous touch.
"I love you" would say too much.
I sing Montaner's rainbow song,
colors glisten like fallen ribbons.
He hears me, smiling softly.
I trace the curve of his lips,
and find him, midbook—
steady—a river drunk on rain,
not as loud as the waterfalls of late,
nor as cutting as the brazen rocks of youth.

Eighteen Years, Going on Forever

How he loves me, it baffles me—
torrential and turbid though I can be,
blunt and sharp when the air stalls
over the cold stone island.
Afraid of speed, slow to shift, yet
mutable—chameleon on brittle leaves.

But it's not all bad, you see.

I can clean, cook, and kiss,
watch an open wound and not flinch,
make nests out of sheds in any season,
wear my Sunday best for no reason…
water thirsty pansies while he's gone,
feign I didn't miss him when he's home.

Threadbare Raw

He wants me softer,
the plush beneath his feet,
no fuzz or drama—
romance in monochrome.
I want him rougher,
so his edges wake my palm,
so I know where he might cut
and where he's smooth
as the valley around his navel.
I kiss him once on the cheek,
and peck his lips, hold
the barren land of his hand in mine,
and breathe. Today isn't the day
I chase sharpness.
Though it pricks—
a blade just shy of skin.

He Wakes Up Early and Leaves

53

Submerged and soured—
tamarind brew of lonely mornings,
bittersweet gulps of embrace.
Silk and lace of bare skin.
I miss you most when you are near,
the hollows of seamless pairings—
dormant when I wake,
alive when I bathe and lather
in the clear boundary between us.
Autumn is for wind, not rain—
falling anew with the streaks
of winter in your hair.

The Day I Learned I Loved Him

You can love someone and not know it,
like the day I almost lost him—
eyes locked, their shared laughter
in a distant kitchen.

Rage, shielding the fear in my ribs.
Knowing myself whole
yet falling through the missing piece.
(Unease) latent in the thorns
of a rose night in winter.

He is far—so far—
and impossibly, he is also here:
subtle, sure,
softening every exhale,
cradling my descent to sleep.

The Tuesday Before the Other Shoe Dropped

Half-lit planets on a dim screen.
The whole Earth fits in my one hand.
9:11 blinks on my lock screen.
An old woman coughs,
slicing through the static.
Across the ocean,
a younger woman trembles—
her lover's month-long silence,
a wilful torture.
He views it as a crescendo of tension,
a triumphant buildup to a sweet reunion.
From where he stands,
he cannot see the frayed cord snapping,
the whip of her acceptance
lashing across his face.

Some people light you up
so you can find your path
without them.

Price of Admission

Even this line takes a tree,
or a measure of its rings,

peeled like old varnish.
Not even thought comes free.

I pay with wistfulness
for sitting under the oak.

I press pennies into its split bark,
drop tears into its pouty mouth,

patch its cracks with sepia leaves—
so I can write of you,

under the umbrella of its grief.

Untranslated

To write about you
in my native language,
I unlearn your tongue.
Not its sounds, or words,
but the splintered, brittle
silence. Idle rubble,
close to bone, mute affections
stuffed in yellow,
time-stained envelopes.
Your eyes, terrifying beams
of night cast over the shrine
of an ancient, dormant sea.

What the Morning Took Back

It wasn't a nightmare—but a dream
within a dream. I woke,
heart pounding, beside you.
I dreamed I lost you and wept.
You smiled, steady as an ancient voyager.
"Everything ends someday.
I'm here now. Close your eyes."
I woke to robins' chattering
unequivocal laments,
a neighbor's car roaring to work,
which sounded more like a cough—
to light searing my eyes,
in and a cold, empty bed.

Winter Pastime

What I learned about us,
we're puzzle pieces that didn't fit—
an imprecision of time and place.
Your desert, my lakes—
an ache for entropy.
Lower still, the abyss…
a purgatory of words that sink,
painting landscapes
from blurry memories,
trying to capture rapture—
in a metaphor.

Paradox of the Attainable

He's so mine that
>I couldn't have him—

a push and pull
>with no discernible rhythm.

His arms, a built-in prison
>wrapped tight around me.

I wanted him more
>than I wanted life.

That was the start
>of my quiet unraveling.

My dreams,   once
>cloudcover and moonglade,

disperse and fade
>over his shadow.

I couldn't fathom life with him…
>the torture of a wish fulfilled.

Words Don't Fade, Dates Don't Lie

Was he a poet?
Your guess is as good as mine—
a maker of virtual worlds,
or simply a dreamer, lost.
He wrote me missives in invisible ink,
long as my legs stretched skyward.
Words became places: home, golden grass.
He turned himself inside out, so I could see
parts of him he didn't know—
extinguished fire, a cigarette
crushed against his arm,
arcane fear of the feminine,
fueling his very tenderness.
A plush bed of soreness—
a viscous web
ruined by mere touch.
When it was time, he let me leave,
swallowing his love—not out of pride.
He left his letters for me to find
on a cold day like this.

Between Stops

Lightning strikes unsuspecting boughs.
I knew the weight of a word
could never pin you down.
You fly through this autumn swirl—
a cinnamon calm, the width of an eye.

I was never astute, but I had moments
when I could shift the breeze to steal a kiss.
I could be the hurricane, not
the shattered ground, discarded rubble
from a life that mattered to someone.

But memory is a train, always passing by
one stop too far from where we were to meet.
You turn transparent, fading from view
as I gaze back through old, fogged glass—
the unscrubbable distance staining my fist.

Landscapes shift from summer to fall,
from city streets to muted country meadows—
painted in swift strokes of watered aquarelle.
I accept love as the base layer of this canvas,
and contentment stirs, faintly, in letting go.

Blue Fire Burn

Those who trade in nostalgia know
the price of an unsaid goodbye.
That the past is the heart's gravity,
pulling with ineluctable weight.
A rose is more fragrant in preterite,
its scent sharper as it fades into thought.
An untouched silhouette rests
deeper and heavier than a warm body.
And fire burns bluer than my tongue,
numb in the frost of an untold winter story.

Parted Waters

Who remembers your eyes
under glaring filters?
A quest in the dense forest
after morning rain.
Who can play the game
when the moment fades,
fickle as ignored daylight?

Nothing's pure
yet we distill its silver
for our crystal ball,
mix it with the aurora
of a thought, and smile.

Who can speak your name
without breaking it, salvage it
from the compost heap
of what once was? Precious
pearls, held by a thief—
vanish from unworthy hands.

Where are you, my love?
When did our waters start to part?
I hold back split sides
of a grave, dead sea,
with outstretched arms.

One Warm Winter

You're late for the unraveling.
Leaves have fallen,
forming a path of colors fading,
mistaken for change.
Follow it, your guide to winter.

Some things are revealed
only in brisk sobriety.
Someone will kiss the frost
from your cheeks,
brush the deadened light
from your eyes as they close.

Dream now, my love.
Someone will plant
their soft, green spring
in your hard, thawing earth.

Under Halley's Tail

What are you now
that the wound is healed?
a softened sigil, pearlescent
under Halley's tail;

an unsung elegy,
musty under the patina
of a languid wish.

What am I now
but aeolian murmur,
soughing on the saddle
of the shifting wind?

What are you if not
an embroidered relic—
a scar that only stirs
before the October rains?

Origami Duck

Place me under your pillow,
that I may remain
an unbidden thought.
Fold me into an origami duck,
to drift on the reflection
of your unshed tears.
Breathe me as untried oxygen,
a wisp of wild chi
to dwell in your lungs.
Write me into your boldest plans,
an untamed shadow character.
I'll stretch myself thin,
ride with the wind that blows.

Overlooked

They won't call when you expect,
or visit when you wish.
They'll arrive empty-handed
to your table, spread for a feast.

Flowers won't blossom
at your command
soon after the last frost.
The ones that do,
you'll overlook.

It's why we revere tulips
over daring daffodils,
no matter how intricate,
or poetic their blooms.

Varnish for a Handmade Fork

An ode to hope,
stubborn and pervasive—
innate malaise
transcending time and space.
Treachery of memory,
varnishing a moment
to lay bare my truth.

This is where I part with you,

unlace the gloves
that touched you softly,
parse the farce
of seamless harmony.
Let the snowflakes slit
the stoic silence.
Let all fall silent,
so the heart can speak.

Leaving it Blank

Everything sleeps
except live-wire nerves.
A grey manna of mist
spoon-feeds emaciated pines.
In contrast, golden grass.
You tell me: Take a nap,
blame it on lack of sleep.

Everything's fine—of course.

I won't rush to fill the silence.
Being awake isn't the challenge.
It's knowing what to think
about the absurd,
what to do about futility,
when to crawl
a crumbling threshold.

Entanglement

Not a single breath is wasted,
not one petal falls silently
on the piercing grass.

Every sigh is a storm,
toppling trees and twirling leaves
three timelines below.

Today I shifted the thinking man
to a smarter spot on the bookshelf.
Suddenly, it dawns on your side.

Tomorrow, I'll die a peaceful death,
far from those who truly love me,
as a lone petal wilts in your kitchen vase.

The Space Between Notes

Surrender isn't the same
as giving up.
It's an octave above
the harmonies we know.

Both are just,
for there is no holy grail
after the quest—
no rich tonality in this dull oneness.

I meet you by the burning bush,
sing you my song
as if you hadn't written it.

You smile wide, pleased,
tell me your story
as if I hadn't lived it, and I nod.

Part III. Stamped in Ash

We are all that we once were,
and we are more.

— *Restoration*

Ancestral Loops

Journey of the seas—
island to island…
Andullos[1] cured by the sun,
packed and rolled
like wilted dreams,
release the scent of home.

I head north, my suitcase light.
I can't carry burdens
on these skinny arms.

You drift above me, or inside—
at this point, who can tell?
I've traveled more than I care to.
Lives turned to detours…
Forking roads collapse,
their ends toward you.

---

[1] **Andullos** are a traditional Dominican tobacco product from the Cibao region: coarsely fermented leaves tightly rolled into dense, sausage-like bundles, wrapped in palm yaguas, pressed, and aged for months to create a strong, aromatic form used for chewing, pipe smoking, or cigar filler, still made artisanally by rural families.

Stamped in Ash

Yesterday, I was a child—
bronzed and bashful,
frail and frog-splashed
in late night serenades.

Taro swamps ran wild
through dusty, open yards.
Ash and embers stamped my calf,
so I wouldn't forget
the kid who pushed me
into the black coal stove.

He's a grown man now,
but I remain a girl,
branded by fire,
yet unburned.

I Know You Can Hear Me

I stopped talking to your golden boy.
I used up the last of your oregano.
I went to the city and rode a boat—
a skyline tour from dock to Liberty.
I didn't share my seat.
I threw away your plastic stirring spoons,
the ones you bought at the dollar store
and left unopened for fifteen years.
I spent a fortune on presents, all for me:
a pair of Uggs, a Manduka mat,
soft and warm stuff, makeup
I'll rarely wear. You catch the drift.
I'm stitching up our wounds: grandma's,
my mother's, yours, and my own.
I spent dearly on the gilded seams.
Messy, uneven, but they seem to hold.

What You Inherit Isn't Stolen

Don't tell her what you do
or where you sometimes go,
chasing a feeling, when peace is
not a place. I saw him in you
when you were a child—his demons
swirling, creeping up your blouse,
smoke beneath your chest.
Guard her innocence
as he once stole yours. Tell her
you're climbing, sightseeing
higher grounds, not trolling
shadows—sinking, like him.

A Gift from Beyond

For my 40th birthday, I had planned a catered party with a Mexican theme in my Illinois home—fajitas and guac, a mariachi and margaritas. Instead, I flew to the Dominican Republic for my father's funeral, and the gift he left me I will carry forever.

In the summer of 2016, I was tending my garden and working on my tan in the Chicago suburbs. After four winters of biting wind and slush, the place had started to feel like home—at least when it thawed. I'd been mulling over how to mark my milestone birthday. A party in the Caribbean tugged at me—with family, at a beach resort—where we wouldn't have to cook or clean. But flying made me anxious, and the planning felt daunting after a draining winter and spring. I've never understood why I despise the cold so much. It's not just the chill, easily countered with layers. It's the heavy, gray shroud that smothers the Midwest sky from November to March, the shovel jammed in wet snow that nearly snapped my wrists, the sting of frozen air seeping through my balaclava on a January walk. So, I settled on a low-effort gathering: a catered party with a handful of friends and a few acquaintances. I wouldn't enjoy it much, but it beat facing my fear.

On the night of June 30, I had a dream too vivid to shake. I was wandering a town—its name unclear—when

I met a couple with a disfigured child, a little girl. They beamed with pride, showing her off as if she were perfect. I didn't ask what was wrong, though curiosity gnawed at me. Later, in the dream, I found her in my house. Startled, I told her she didn't belong there.

The next morning, around 11 a.m., my family's WhatsApp chat lit up. Dad had been rushed to intensive care from dialysis. His blood had cycled through those machines for twelve years—far longer than the three-to-five-year average for most patients. My mother was his lifeline, sitting beside him at every session, monitoring his blood pressure, befriending the nurses to ensure he got the best care. We credited her devotion, and the love that surrounded him, for his endurance. Isn't that the secret to a long life—being needed, cherished? That day, reading the messages, my dream clicked into place. The little girl was me, and my father, eighty-two, was dying. My brother called soon after to confirm it. I booked the flight home.

On the two plane rides, I talked nonstop with the strangers beside me—a tribute to my affable dad. My fear of flying vanished. Nothing could touch me while I raced to him. At the funeral home, I sank my fingers into his doughy arm, swollen from years of dialysis needles and water retention. I kissed his large, cold forehead. My beautiful dad—not some heartthrob, though I'd tease him he looked sixteen, just to see him smirk. Beautiful because he was gentle, fierce in protecting his children, glowering at anyone who dared look at us with less than kindness.

84

He was proud of us, all seven (eight, counting the stillborn). A priest once warned him too many kids would ruin him. "Watch me," he'd replied. Sacristan by morning, candle maker and barber by afternoon, he gave us more than enough. He built a loving home, a sanctuary for study and play, an open door that welcomed everyone. He taught us that sharing our little meant Providence would provide. And it did: one priest, one nun, two lawyers, an accountant, and two black sheep in the land of the free—myself included—independent and (mostly) brave. Whatever we became after leaving town, we will always be known as "*los hijos de Blas*" (Blas' kids): raised with care and highly protected by a no-nosense, God-fearing man.

The church in Jarabacoa, where my dad worked for over thirty years, where I swept the floors and dusted the pews every Saturday, overflowed for his service. The town drunk, the local eccentric, clergy, businessmen, old friends, extended family—everyone came. The country's vice-president and her entourage showed up too, partly because of my sister's standing, but mostly because she'd met my dad and took a liking to him. Five hundred people might fit inside, but through swollen, tear-blurred eyes, I saw more crowding in the back. In that moment, I understood my father's final gift: a revelation of a life well-lived, measured by the love bursting through the hurricane shutters, and the respect of everyone who knew him, rising from the soaring ceiling to the boundless, clear sky.

Prayer as a Child-Rearing Tool

She was five when I pushed her
on the bike without training wheels.
The bike moved freely, unlike the wall
now rising between us, brick by brick.
I still push; I can't stop.
This is what my mother tells me:
that children possess intensity,
but no hindsight—so my hands
must press against her walls,
gently and patiently, until they fall—
or clasp together in prayer.

Between Puberty and Menopause

Mothers are magicians
without tricks,
swaying to the hum
of mismatched frequencies.
No matter what I do,
I will be blamed for something:
a failure to launch,
overreaching, underloving,
water beads on her collar
as she dances in the rain.

Joy

She tells me the *Minecraft* movie
reshaped her world, sparked a hunger
to skydive. I spin my tale of paragliding,
the wind, our friend over soaring hills.

She orders French toast, piled high
with strawberries—bananas shoved aside.
I choose The Kitchen Sink for sausage links,
creamy grits, and a bit of everything.

She calls life a book series, some tomes rushed,
ink-smudged, and shaky plots. I share
I used to die dreaming at her age, drinking
"Morir Soñando" (milk swirled with orange juice).

A Mother is Supposed to Know Things

How inadequate, my voice
telling her it was just a dream.
No one will chase her with a knife.
I, too, have nightmares—
fringe illusions, obscure fears—
too irrational for daylight:
strangers invading my home,
a disfigured child, who turned out to be me,
the night before my father died
without saying goodbye.
I had seen her on the streets.
Her parents, doting on her,
so proud. Why? I wondered,
can't they see her horrid face?
Someone will chase my child, alright,
though not with the proverbial knife.
A thought that hunts itself will find her,
unsuspecting, unarmed.
Her only weapon, what she lets in.
Her saving grace, what she let go.

The Acoustics of Tension

I hold her hand as we cross
the busy street—a squeeze.
She trusts me now to keep her safe.
It wasn't always this way.
Squirrels prance across the road,
a crunch—magnolia leaves bounce,
relics of yesteryear. Cicadas cheer us
uphill—a shrill. Droning whirs,
soft buzzing, a crow's caw splitting
the damp air. There's only room for one
queen in the hive. So we buzz, and
we bump—like worker bees in the hum.

When the Student Is Ready…

I was once a player; now I mentor
a girl in the survival show. She chose me,
as every initiate selects their sage.
What I can teach her—I'm not sure.
I only ever learned from Solitude,
cloaked as a fragile damsel,
not in distress but always scheming.
Today, she packs her wisdom, tight and dry,
into a sandbag, then sews it shut.
A deluge will come—it always does.
Afterward, we'll go home.

Keep it Light, It's 2025

"How did you sleep, my love?"
I took an Advil—well, Kirkland-brand
acetaminophen, but does it matter?
I slept great. Not hungover anymore
from the one shot of premium rum,
a flute of Prosecco, and half a beer
from two nights ago (New Year's Eve).
This morning, I heated a slice
of banana bread I baked last night,
brewed fresh coffee in my Italian maker.
Later, I'll break in my new yoga mat—
75 minutes with Travis—breath work and sweat,
pleasure, pain, without leaving home.
Outside, the northern chill swallows
the morning crisp—frigid, but bright.
I won't lie, I'm still hungover
from one too many laughs
with my sisters on WhatsApp,
and that one conversation (eye roll)
with the drunk Freud wannabe
who drowns everything in tears
when all I want is chuckles,
or at least a light chat:
banana bread, casseroles,
alien invasions, nine dimensions,
crypto scammers and whatnot.

Exiled in the Sky

At commencement, they called us
"citizens of the world."
I looked around and thought…
Yes, we come from every place,
yet citizens, we are not.
We are exotic birds,
nesting in no-man's land,
soaring 'cause we have wings
(and broken feet).

Restoration

Because we are more than convicts
sent to sea to escape their fate,
or find it on an island. Because we are
more than the natives who inhabited it,
with gold in their hands, and ground achiote
on their faces. Because we are more
than slaves, servile then rebellious,
stacking bricks on the master's ochre dreams.
Because more than mulattos or mestizos,
we are brothers. We are more than
newcomers to a brown land.
We are more than the tricolor mantle that hangs
from our shoulders to our feet.
We are all that we once were,
and we are more... much more.

To Oust A Dictator

If everything else is a lie,
the poetry must be true
in this game of makeshift histories.
An ocean of a crowd
rushes to the open shore.
A single voice resounds
like a stone in the void.
Consent to the noise,
it will deafen you stoically.
A bad man holds the torch
and snuffs it out by hand.
He knows he's no victor,
yet on his charred throne, he sits.

A Witch Is Getting Married Today

Tomorrow, always tomorrow…
We close our eyes under the rain's caress,
rivers rushing down our cheeks and necks—
plunging sheers of cellophane.
A young Madonna with flawless skin sings—
mauve lips and a jet black pixie cut,
mediterranean eyes lost in tropical blues.
Her manicured, restless hands trace the outline
of her jaw. "Here comes the sun," she hums
as the stage splits open in a flood of light.
And the islander in me would say:
a witch is getting married today—
her veil spun from sunlight and rain,
her faint smile, a nod to the moment.

Part IV. In Every New Beginning

Her saving grace, what she let go.

— *A Mother is Supposed to Know Things*

Late Summer Breakfast

I turn my face away
from the swollen self,
spoon-fed, green and wet,
with pity and doubt.
My neck cracks—
my eyes shout.

Outside the window,
goldfinches gorge
on the dry heart
of a withered Denver Daisy,
so lithely, so softly
the stem doesn't move.

sleeping seeds wake soft
mother moon hums languidly
there's still time to grow

Born to Use the Senses

Follow the track of modest light,
a narrow path out of the dense forest,
where foolish youth is no roadblock,
nor ripe age, liberation.
Do not chase pine-scented footfalls
into the deepest wilderness,
where land sinks into a gorge,
and the river never runs.
We were born for the city
of unsketched skylines
and unheeded thoughts—
for croissants and morning coffee,
high-top sneakers and whatnot.

Facetiming to a New Landscape

As if the snow were elastic,
he springs north, points at bare mountains
we could tread with swaddled legs.
He will pull me upward when my lungs quit,
reveal the mercy of a topaz sky—
after I tore the old one at the seams
to uncover something beyond
a faded landscape I had no wish to repaint.

He hikes six miles through ice and slush,
calls me when the thought of it thaws.
After all, he is the goat,
surefooted on sketchy climbs, and I,
the fair-weather river crab.
Once more, we hope: this will be home—
a nest at high altitude for
creatures without wings—
a tangle of want, and will.

From Up Here

Of all the things that hold power
over tired eyes, the September haze
dispersing across red rock.
He points toward a clearing,
a vastness that is our domain—
shared with sheep and lamb,
torn from the feeble night.
A wolf drifts, howling
through the red sea of a blood moon,
disoriented without its pack.
I stop. The breeze, a wrapper
around my tender back.
I've never seen you in this light—
no oak, no pine
to shadow your contours.

cloudy winter day
a pink trash truck rolls slowly
thrill of letting go

Here At Last

And home dawns as a quiet ache
after years tangled in a pungent maze.
My eyes well, recognizing the long way here,
as if losing myself were an affront,
time scattered on barren flatlands
like sterile seed.

One foot before the next,
mapping unnecessary journeys—
penance to the god of foolishness,
paid in the currency of youth.

Snow rejected me
when I looked at it sideways.
The southern sun burned me
seven years too long.

But here at last,
under the tutelage of still-green giants,
I sit.

Pilot Light

There is a ripening born of coldness,
a balmy palette worn with age.
A yellowing engulfs
the elasticity of dancing grass.
This warmth in view is a warning.

I avert my eyes to the faithful blue—
why, the sky is always true.
Pass what may beneath it,
churn what may above it,
it will not mature.

Such is the nature of the ethereal—
what we aspire to be:
even turning blue from the cold,
our pilot light stays on.

Reuse. Recycle

Addicted to form...
What I ignore dissolves
behind my back.
Earth swallows it
with spring rain.

It floods, pools at my feet.
I stomp in the muck,
abandon my shoes.

Nothing stays unused.
A muddy shoe becomes home
for bugs and worms.
A leaning arm, a trellis
for a climbing rose.

And the heart, a barrel
brimming with unfallen rain.

The Dream of Self

Does the tree feel the mountain?
Does it know itself
beyond the ground that holds it?

Does it imagine walking—
shaking loose its roots,
tiptoeing downhill
through the blur of night?

In the meadow below,
it dreams an oasis:
itself at the center,
a bench for a squirrel's pause.

Its orange leaves,
also leaving,
forging their own dream:
a single flight to their end,
a languid, jubilant descent.

What Each Hand Knows

It is my left hand that builds,
picking, shoveling, hammering—
holding flame to stone,
shaping clay, sanding fine edges.
It's the hand that holds the diamonds
prickling my chest and ears,
just to feel their weight,
colorless and valued
like a hard-fought past.

My right hand writes—
index finger parting air
into unseen commands,
coloring my pale lips
two tones happier,
reaching empty to receive
daisies not bought,
planted or watered,
but gifted because I asked,
palm up and open—
misty eyes refracting light.

Happy Old Hag

One more dream
of upside-down smiles
painted in rainbows,

mystical pools
where our skin dissolves
in sulfuric landscapes.

With you—without you—
life laughs

like a crowned hyena,
at last embraced
by those who once despised her...

thunderous as a phantom at dusk—
not quite feared,
not quite loved.

Lightening the Load

Everything is neat, at last.
Poetry books are stashed
away from prying eyes.
I desire nothing but a bed
spread on a shaded stretch of meadow,
a touch of sunlight on my chest
when I turn to watch the trees—
for a moment of wonderment
before falling asleep,
with nothing else asked of me.

Restlessness—insatiable as dreams.
I toss and turn until dawn's first blink.
Spring tumbles in, leafing timidly,
blooming wildly in the periphery—
a baby yellow, a misty pink
reigning, ephemerally
over the unyielding, pewter weight
of everything that stays the same.

Us, Preserved in Amber

Down a slope,
a hush of downy white,
a wonder of blues and pine.
You appear
like a fatigued memory
before the pain.
A fossil in the stillness,
amber in the rapture
of a dying twilight.
This, I know, is us—
a fracture of life and thought…
Thunder in the valley,
wonder at the crest,
sonder in the lull
of a breath.

Tender with Teeth

I am soft,
too soft for the world sometimes—
pensive peach-pineapple pulp,
eaten in one big gulp.

My hands know this.
They curl into fists,
primed to attack.
"Relax," I tell them.

We are safe here:
cooking simple meals
in a kitchen I loathe to clean,
loving the scrape of soap on steel,

a neighborhood unruly
with children's screams,
bubbly clouds tickling the mellow sky.
"I could lie on them," I whisper,
"and you could braid their cotton mane
while I nap."

They nod. I lean back,
quiet settling over me.
But clouds are too plush—
too soft for me sometimes.

Every New Beginning

Another life waits beyond—
a wrinkled dress unworn,
clean hair swept up,
lips brushed in peach and hush.
Flowers still blooming
since last spring,
the sky an even-tempered blue.
A glimpse—his gaze
disarms my weary face,
a blush of scarlet
on my never innocence.
His shadow tilts
my every noon,
his fingers contour
my every landscape.

Goals

To take the measure
of my life on your palm,
and find no trace of my name.

To stretch my lines beyond
time's blurred margins,
like an epic—unread, unknown.

To lay your smile
across a forgotten meadow,
wheat and golden grass
weeping a distant song.

To remain—not with you,
but within you—
tame, halting mornings,

wild, hand-fed nights,
tattering the hems
of your fine-pressed suit.

To paint the last light with you…

fresh, slow ascension
warm air sates my empty lungs
I glide on a breath

Over the Hill

No sound but breath,
no depth but thoughts
undulating through static.
Mountains sway,
shoulder to shoulder, green,
bearing the weight of the unseen.
Nostalgia, palpable yet useless,
creeps like cotton clouds
in a jute basket. I sleep on it
until my heart, a child,
peekabooes over the hill.
There you are—
slow-pulsing a bright new day,
dreaming a brand-new life.

The Secret

The secret is there is no secret.
The sea makes waves because it's restless.
Without the storm, it would have nowhere to go.
Somewhere in the mountains, a cry goes unheard,
a group hug unfelt, aspens bound as one.
Fell one in autumn's blaze, the others will shiver—
weeping beneath their cooling breath.
Roots tingle through winter.
By spring, another shoots upward,
new branches stretch to reclaim the void,
leaves mumbling prayers as you pass.
The secret is… we endure.

Verve

A river too young for its bed
sleeps in the nearby valley.
It calls it freedom. We call it flood.

The wind blows through the city—
nothing in the desert to slap against.
We call it gutsy. It calls it fun.

No one wants to sing our song
since we hid behind the curtains.
We call that luck.

And to know that someday,
through no fault of our own,
we'll be estranged from all we love—

not as punishment,
but as rite of passage,
because a tree needs The Hanged Man.

We see the world upside down,
as if for the first time,
yet we know this place—

we know where the river bends
and meets its shallow end.
We call it sea.

The Vanishing Point

It begins when random voices start
to rhyme—not with sound, but thought—
a crescendoing cadence
for those who hear the drums.
I lose you in this hum, where orphaned
souls are commonplace. When I find you,
it's not your face, not your eyes,
yet still, you see me, still, you smile
an implicit promise to begin again.

And when it ends, it ends. I look for
landmarks to find my bearings.
The anticlimax of our twinned fates
is easy to spot. An eagle breaches
the depressed horizon and disappears
midflight, swallowed by the yawning sun.
I pronounce you dead by twilight,
name myself Glory, a hollow title,
but mine to embody. The drums beat again,
deep within my ears—a stranger's hand
reaches for mine, and I take it.

About the Author

Antonia Wang is a poet whose work explores intimacy, time, memory, and the quiet forces that shape a life. Writing across languages and emotional geographies, her poems examine what endures, what dissolves, and what remains when certainty falls away.

She is the author of eleven poetry collections—eight original works in English, including *The Constant*, and three in Spanish—each tracing a different phase of inner and relational evolution. *The Constant* continues this unfolding body of work, reflecting a deepening inquiry into permanence, change, and the stories we carry forward.

Antonia's books are available through booksellers worldwide in print and digital formats.

Acknowledgements

The following haiku were published in Tranquility: An Anthology of Haiku by Literary Revelations in April 2025. My thanks to its editor, Gabriela Marie Milton, for sharing my work:

park bench reverie - page 30
watercolor rain - page 38
sleeping seeds wake soft - page 102
cloudy winter day - page 106
fresh, slow ascension - page 118

I am deeply grateful to the journals and editors who have published my writing, to the #vss365 Writing Community on X, and to my readers for their support.